D1266555

Nebraska

Jim Ollhoff

Visit us at
www.abdopublishing.com

Published by ABDO Publishing Company, 8000 West 78th Street, Suite 310, Edina, Minnesota 55439 USA. Copyright ©2010 by Abdo Consulting Group, Inc. International copyrights reserved in all countries. No part of this book may be reproduced in any form without written permission from the publisher. The Checkerboard Library™ is a trademark and logo of ABDO Publishing Company.

Printed in the United States.

Editor: John Hamilton
Graphic Design: Sue Hamilton
Cover Illustration: Neil Klinepier
Cover Photo: iStock
Interior Photo Credits: Alamy, AP Images, Comstock, Corbis, Getty, Granger Collection, iStock Photo, Independence National Historical Park/Artist-C.W. Peale, Jimmy Emerson, Library of Congress, Mile High Maps, Mountain High Maps, Nichole-Flickr, North Wind Picture Archives, One Mile Up, Peter Arnold Inc., Smithsonian Institute, United States Air Force, and United States National Park Service.
Statistics: State population statistics taken from 2008 U.S. Census Bureau estimates. City and town population statistics taken from July 1, 2007, U.S. Census Bureau estimates. Land and water area statistics taken from 2000 Census, U.S. Census Bureau.

Manufactured with paper containing at least 10% post-consumer waste

Library of Congress Cataloging-in-Publication Data

Ollhoff, Jim, 1959-
 Nebraska / Jim Ollhoff.
    p. cm. -- (The United States)
 Includes index.
 ISBN 978-1-60453-662-1
 1. Nebraska--Juvenile literature. I. Title.

 F666.3.O39 2010
 978.2--dc22

                                      2008051718

Table of Contents

The Cornhusker State

In 1820, Major Stephen Long came back from exploring the Great Plains. He believed that the area of present-day Nebraska was a desert. A mapmaker of the time labeled the area as "The Great Desert." Lewis and Clark said Nebraska was the same as the Sahara Desert of Africa. They were all very wrong.

Today, Nebraska is a land where hard-working farmers grow food for the nation. Nebraska is full of people who love their state, and they love their history. They also love their university football team, the Cornhuskers.

Modern Nebraska is a major food-producing state. It is the place where yesterday's frontier and today's farmland meet.

A rainbow forms over
a Nebraska cornfield.

Quick Facts

Name: The word "Nebraska" comes from an Oto (a Native American tribe) term meaning "flat water," a reference to the Platte River.

State Capital: Lincoln, population 248,744

Date of Statehood: March 1, 1867 (37th state)

Population: 1,783,432 (38th-most populous state)

Area (Total Land and Water): 77,354 square miles (200,346 sq km), 16th-largest state

Largest City: Omaha, population 424,482

Nickname: The Cornhusker State

Motto: Equality Before the Law

State Bird: Western Meadowlark

State Flower: Goldenrod

State Tree: Cottonwood

State Song: "Beautiful Nebraska"

Highest Point: Panorama Point in southwestern Kimball County, 5,424 feet (1,653 m)

Lowest Point: Southeastern Richardson County at the Missouri River, 840 feet (256 m)

Average July Temperature: 73°F (23°C) in the far west, to 78°F (26°C) in the southeast

Record High Temperature: 118°F (48°C)

Average January Temperature: 24°F (-4°C) in the west, to 20°F (-7°C) in the northeast

Record Low Temperature: -47°F (-44°C)

Missouri River

Average Annual Precipitation: 33 inches (84 cm) in the southeast to less than 16 inches (41 cm) in the west

Number of U.S. Senators: 2

Number of U.S. Representatives: 3

Gerald Ford

U.S. Presidents Born in Nebraska: Gerald Ford, 38th president

U.S. Postal Service Abbreviation: NE

Geography

Nebraska is about 210 miles (338 km) from north to south, and about 430 miles (692 km) from east to west. With an area of 77,354 square miles (200,346 sq km), Nebraska is the 16th-largest state.

Nebraska is a part of the United States called the Great Plains. Plains means "flat land." There might be gently sloping hills, but it is mostly flat. On the plains, there are fewer trees than in many states. This flat land is good for farming.

Nebraskans take advantage of their rich soil and flat land. More than 93 percent of Nebraska is used for farming or ranching. The eastern side of the state is mostly used for farming. The western side of the state is good ranch land for raising cattle and other animals.

NEBRASKA

SOUTH DAKOTA

MINNESOTA

IOWA

WYOMING

COLORADO

KANSAS

MISSOURI

North Platte River

Missouri River

Platte River

North Platte

Grand Island

Omaha

Lincoln

N

0   100 miles
0   100 km

Nebraska's total land and water area is 77,354 square miles (200,346 sq km). It is the 16th-largest state. The state capital is Lincoln.

Much of the water used for farming comes from the Ogallala Aquifer. An aquifer is a large pool of underground water. It is easily pumped out of the ground. The Ogallala Aquifer is very large. It is below the ground of eight central states, including Nebraska. It is very important for Nebraska agriculture.

The Missouri River played an important role in settling the West. Lewis and Clark followed the Missouri River on their journey to the Pacific Ocean. The Platte River also played an important role in history. Settlers followed the 310-mile (499-km) Platte River on their westward journeys. Many pioneers crossed Nebraska using landmarks like Chimney Rock and Scotts Bluff National Monument.

Nebraska has more than 11,000 miles (17,703 km) of rivers. Nebraska is one of the states with the most mileage in rivers. More than 2,500 lakes, both natural and artificial, dot the state.

A buffalo and cattle share grazing space near Chimney Rock. Thousands of pioneers used Chimney Rock as a landmark when crossing Nebraska.

Climate and Weather

Nebraskans live with weather extremes. Each year, hailstorms, thunderstorms, and blizzards hit the state. Nebraska sees an average of 37 tornadoes every year. People in the state live with very hot summers and very cold winters.

Temperatures can change quickly when cold winds shoot down from the north. The weather can also change when hot winds blow from the southwest. Temperatures have changed 50 degrees Fahrenheit (10°C) in one day.

Summer temperatures are often between 90 degrees Fahrenheit (32°C) to 100 degrees Fahrenheit (38°C). Winter brings cold air down from Canada. Temperatures can often fall below 0 degrees Fahrenheit (-18°C). Blizzards bring strong winds that whip across the plains.

A tornado one-mile (1.6-km) wide threatens north-central Nebraska.

Plants and Animals

Grass is the most common plant in Nebraska. In eastern Nebraska, bluestem grass is common. Bluestem grass is a tall prairie grass. Shorter grasses, like buffalo grass, are more common in the west. Flowers are everywhere. Goldenrod, columbine, wild roses, and sunflowers are common types of flowers. Wild plums and chokecherries can also be found throughout Nebraska.

Chokecherries

Only three percent of Nebraska was forested when the first European-American settlers came. Tree planting has become important. Arbor Day began in Nebraska. Today, ash, cottonwood, oak, elm, and willow trees are found in the central and eastern side of the state. Pine and cedar are more common in the west.

Wildflowers on Nebraska grasslands.

There are many kinds of animals in Nebraska. Deer, prairie dogs, coyotes, muskrats, raccoons, rabbits, skunks, and squirrels can be found almost anywhere.

Large herds of buffalo roamed Nebraska until hunters almost killed them all. Today in Nebraska, buffalo are only found in wildlife refuges. Beavers were also almost wiped out by early hunters, but have made a comeback.

The most common fish in Nebraska are bass, crappie, catfish, perch, carp, pike, trout, and walleye. Game birds are found throughout Nebraska, including ducks, geese, quail, and pheasants.

Bobwhite Quail

The world's largest groups of sandhill cranes can be found each spring in central Nebraska, in the Platte River Valley. Almost a half-million birds stop to rest as they travel south for the winter.

A buffalo in Nebraska's Fort Niobrara National Wildlife Refuge.

Prairie Dog

Rabbit

Sandhill Crane

History

Humans were in Nebraska 10,000 years ago, and probably much earlier than that. The early peoples were nomadic. They hunted herds of animals.

A Native American earthen lodge.

From 1600 to 1800, there were many Native American tribes in today's Nebraska. In the east, the Oto, Pawnee, Ponca, and Omaha people lived in earthen lodges. They grew much of their own food. In the west, the Lakota and Cheyenne lived in teepees and hunted. The Comanche, Arapaho, and Oglala Sioux also lived in the western half of Nebraska. By 1800, the population of Nebraska was about 40,000.

An 1833 Karl Bodmer painting of a young Omaha boy with pierced ears.

The first European to see today's Nebraska was a Frenchman named Étienne Veniard de Bourgmont. In 1714, he traveled the Missouri River to the mouth of the Platte River. In 1739, two brothers, Pierre and Paul Mallet, explored Nebraska. They traveled down the Platte River, exploring almost the entire length of the state.

All through the 1700s, Spain and France tried to claim the land. In 1803, France sold a large amount of land, including Nebraska, to the United States. This was called the Louisiana Purchase.

Lincoln, Nebraska, is named after Abraham Lincoln.

In the 1840s, many people traveled across Nebraska to reach lands in the far West. Many chose to stay in Nebraska. In 1854, Nebraska became a territory of the United States.

Many Native Americans were killed by disease and warfare. Over the next few decades, the Native American tribes were forced to live on small reservations.

Nebraska became a state on March 1, 1867. Leaders moved the capital to the city of Lancaster. They renamed the city "Lincoln," in honor of President Abraham Lincoln.

Wagon trains cross the Nebraska plains.

By the 1880s, railroads crisscrossed the state. More settlers came to Nebraska.

A Nebraska farm family stands in front of a sod house in 1886.

Farmers had good years and bad years. In the 1880s, grasshopper swarms, droughts, and conflicts between ranchers and farmers made life difficult. Still, people knew there were many opportunities in Nebraska. They stayed even during hard times. By 1890, more than one million people lived in Nebraska.

During World War I (1914-1918), more than 47,000 Nebraskans left their homes to fight in Europe. A new demand for food products during the war created many jobs for Nebraska farmers.

After World War I, the need for Nebraska's farming products slowed. The start of the Great Depression in 1929 hit the state's farmers very hard. Many farmers lost their land.

During the 1930s, things slowly improved. When the United States entered World War II in 1941, the need for farming products grew again. This greatly helped Nebraska farmers.

New technology to water crops helped farmers in the years after World War II. Machinery made farming easier, so farms became bigger.

Rows and rows of soybeans on a Nebraska farm.

Did You Know?

In 1971, Dr. Michael Voorhies, was out walking with his wife. He was a paleontologist, a scientist who studies fossils. He was walking through a series of gullies in northeast Nebraska. He thought erosion from heavy rains might have exposed some fossils. He came upon some rhinoceros bones.

As he dug, he uncovered one of the best fossil beds in the country. Camels, horses, deer, and rhinoceroses were crowded into the site. What made the fossil bed unusual is that the bones were all connected. In most fossil beds, the bones have been torn apart by predators.

What Dr. Voorhies had discovered was an ancient watering hole. A volcano in present-day Idaho had erupted, filling the air with toxic smoke, dust, and rock.

While these animals were in the watering hole, the air was filled with choking dust and smoke. Ash quickly covered the dead animals. They became fossilized after lying undisturbed for 10 million years.

A museum was built around the bones. The Ashfall Fossil Beds State Historical Park is near Royal, Nebraska.

Dr. Michael Voorhies of the University of Nebraska with bones of a 10 million-year-old horse and 25 million-year-old Oreodont, a small sheep-like mammal.

People

Johnny Carson (1925-2005) was a famous TV talk show host for nearly 30 years. Carson was born in Iowa, but moved to Norfolk, Nebraska,

when he was eight years old. Carson graduated from the University of Nebraska in 1949. He got his start working on radio and then TV in Nebraska. In 1950, he moved to California. Carson worked on several TV shows, before taking the job as host of *The Tonight Show* in 1962. He interviewed thousands of movie and TV personalities, as well as other interesting people. Carson earned many awards, and became known as the King of Late Night TV.

Grace Abbott (1878-1939) was born in Grand Island, Nebraska. After attending high school and college in Nebraska, she began to work with immigrant children. She became a leader who protected children's rights. She was the head of the Children's Bureau of the United States Department of Labor.

Susan La Flesche Picotte (1865-1915) was born on an Omaha Reservation in Nebraska. Her father was Chief Joseph La Flesche, the last chief of his tribe. As a child, she saw a women in her tribe die. She decided to become a doctor so she could treat her people. In 1889, she became the first Native American woman to become a medical doctor in the U.S.

Standing Bear (1829-1908) was a Native American Ponca chief, born in northeast Nebraska. His tribe was removed from their lands in 1877. They were forced to walk to a reservation in Oklahoma. They arrived too late in the year to plant crops. Many of his people died. Several newspapers wrote about the terrible treatment of the Ponca people. Standing Bear argued in court that Native Americans should have all the rights of white people. The judge agreed with Standing Bear, and his people were freed immediately. Today, Standing Bear is buried on a hill overlooking the place of his birth.

Warren Buffet (1930-) is a businessperson and investor. He was born in Omaha, Nebraska. In 2007, he was ranked as the second-richest person in the world (Bill Gates was the first). He is the head of a company called Berkshire Hathaway. He has given much of his fortune to charity. Despite his fantastic wealth, about $37 billion in 2009, he lives in the same house he bought in 1958 in Omaha.

Cities

Omaha is the largest city in Nebraska. Its population is 424,482. The city is named after the Native American

The Missouri River runs by Omaha, Nebraska

Omaha tribe that used to live in the area. The railroad to the western states began in Omaha, so it became a center of trade and industry. Today, Omaha is the largest meat-packing center in the world. It is also home to many major corporations, including Mutual of Omaha, ConAgra Foods, and Union Pacific Railroad.

The city of **Lincoln** is named in honor of President Abraham Lincoln. It is the capital of Nebraska and the second-largest city. Its population is 248,744. Lincoln became an important railroad junction between 1870 and 1890. The city remains a center of farm products. It is also home to many businesses and manufacturers. Lincoln is home to the University of Nebraska.

A statue of Abraham Lincoln stands in front of Nebraska's state capital building.

Grand Island was started in the 1850s. A group of people set out from Davenport, Iowa, to start a town in central Nebraska. They believed that central Nebraska would be a good stopping place for future railroads. They settled in a place along the Platte River,

near an island that the French traders called "La Grande Island." When the railroads came through in 1868, the town grew rapidly. Today, Grand Island is the fourth-largest city in Nebraska, with a population of 44,802.

Hall County Courthouse in Grand Island, Nebraska.

Bill Cody's home, Scout's Rest, is now a state park in North Platte.

North Platte is located where the North Platte River and the South Platte River join to form the Platte River. It was plotted to be a city along the railroad to the West, and it was organized in 1874. Buffalo Bill Cody (1846-1917) lived in North Platte, and his ranch is now a state historical park. North Platte is also the home of the world's largest railroad yard, called Bailey Yard. The city's population is 24,079.

Transportation

In the late 1800s, Nebraska was heavily traveled by people heading west. Pioneers and settlers often traveled along the Platte River. When the Transcontinental Railroad came through Nebraska, it followed much of the same trail as the pioneers took.

Today, Interstate I-80 follows roughly the same route. It is a major east-west road for the nation.

I-80 runs under the Archway Monument, a tourist stop near Kearney, Nebraska.

Railroads came early to the state. They provided a way for farmers and ranchers to get their products to market. Railroads are still important for transportation in Nebraska.

The two primary commercial airports in Nebraska are Lincoln Airport and Omaha's Eppley Airfield.

Other commercial airports are found in Kearney, Grand Island, North Platte, and Scottsbluff. There are more than 80 smaller airports, plus a large military airfield at Offutt Air Force Base in Sarpy County, near Omaha.

People watch as a jumbo jet carrying the space shuttle *Atlantis* lands for refueling at Offutt Air Force Base near Omaha, Nebraska.

Natural Resources

The most important natural resource in Nebraska is the soil. The eastern side of Nebraska has rich, fertile soil that is excellent for growing crops. The western side of Nebraska has good land for ranches, with plentiful grasses for animals to graze.

Nebraska's largest agricultural crop is corn. More than eight million acres (3.2 million ha) are planted with corn. Most of the corn is fed to the state's livestock and poultry. Nebraska has been first in the nation in producing Great Northern beans. Nebraska was third among the states in sorghum, sixth in soybeans, and sixth in alfalfa. Other crops include winter wheat, sugar beets, popcorn, and wild hay.

There are more than 47,600 farms in the state. The average size of a farm in Nebraska is about 953 acres (386 ha). The ranches and farms are home to more than 6.5 million cattle, and 3 million hogs and pigs.

There is some mining in the state, mostly to produce cement, crushed rock, and gravel.

Nebraska has many farms and ranches.

Industry

Agriculture is the most important industry in Nebraska. Manufacturing and selling machinery for farms is also important.

Lincoln employs many people in education. The University of Nebraska is in the city. Omaha is a major center for food processing, insurance, and health care.

Large private employers in Nebraska include Tyson Foods, Walmart, and the Union Pacific Railroad. ConAgra, located in Omaha, is one of the largest flour millers in the nation.

The largest public employers are the state and federal governments. The U.S. Air Force, primarily at the Offutt Air Force Base near Omaha, employs about 12,000 people.

Tourism is becoming more important in Nebraska. Visitors can explore the trail of Lewis and Clark, or walk in the footsteps of those who took covered wagons across the Oregon Trail. Western Nebraska has beautiful cliffs and bluffs. They are popular with sightseers.

Scotts Bluff is a natural landmark and path marker for travelers.

Sports

Nebraska has no major league sports teams. However, it is home to the Omaha Royals, a minor league baseball team. Another minor league baseball team is the Lincoln Saltdogs. The Omaha Beef is a member of the Indoor Football League.

State residents have a passion for the University of Nebraska's college football team, the Nebraska Cornhuskers.

The Nebraska Cornhuskers, from the University of Nebraska, is a popular college football team.

The Cornhuskers football team won its first game in 1890. Since 1970, the team has won five national championships. The University of Nebraska also competes in 14 other sports.

Nebraska has 87 state parks, recreation areas, and historic parks. Hiking, biking, and canoeing are popular.

Western Nebraska includes Scotts Bluff National Monument and Chimney Rock National Historic Site. Early pioneers used these landmarks as guides. They informed the travelers that they were on the correct trail.

Horseback riders atop Red Cloud Buttes overlook Nebraska's Fort Robinson State Park.

Entertainment

Omaha's Henry Doorly Zoo is one of the finest in the United States. Spread over 130 acres (53 ha), it is home to 17,000 animals. It includes 44 endangered species and 7 threatened species. It has the world's largest indoor rainforest and desert buildings.

Desert Dome at the Henry Doorly Zoo in Omaha is the world's largest indoor replica of a desert.

A huge event in the state is Nebraskaland Days. It celebrates Nebraska's land and culture. It is held for almost two weeks every June.

The center of the celebration is in North Platte. More than 100,000 people crowd into town for rodeos, concerts, art shows, parades, and sporting events.

The Sheldon Memorial Art Gallery in Lincoln has more than 12,000 works of art. These include many kinds of art, from sculptures to paintings. Omaha's Joslyn Art Museum has 11,000 works of art from all over the world. It is famous for its art of the Old West.

Museums, local theaters, and art festivals fill the

state. Examples of Nebraska's rich diversity include the Czech Festival in Wilber, Native American powwows, and the Cowboy Capital of Ogallala.

A rodeo event during Nebraskaland Days.

Timeline

1714—Étienne Veniard de Bourgmont is the first European in Nebraska.

1803—The French sell Nebraska (included in the Louisiana Purchase) to the United States.

1804—Lewis and Clark travel up the Missouri River and explore present-day Nebraska.

1820—The first U.S. Army military post in Nebraska is established at Fort Atkinson.

1822—First permanent settlement of European-Americans at Bellevue.

 **1840s**—Settlers by the tens of thousands travel through Nebraska.

 **1867**—Nebraska becomes the 37th state on March 1, 1867.

 **1867**—Lincoln becomes the state capital (replacing Omaha).

 **1877**— Oglala Sioux leader Crazy Horse surrenders, along with 1,000 of his followers, near Fort Robinson, Nebraska.

 **1948**—The U.S. Strategic Air Command opens near Omaha.

 **2002**—Desert Dome, the world's largest indoor desert, opens at Omaha's Henry Doorly Zoo.

Glossary

Aquifer—Water that is underground, in the dirt and rock. Unlike an underground river in a cave, an aquifer is water that is saturated in the ground—like a kitchen sponge. Water can be pumped out for irrigation and other uses. Part of the immense Ogallala Aquifer is underneath Nebraska.

Arbor Day—A day set aside for planting trees in the United States and other countries. It usually takes place in April or May.

Erosion—When winds or rains wash away the soil.

Louisiana Purchase—A large area of land in North America purchased from France in 1803. The land went from the Mississippi River to the Rocky Mountains and from the Gulf of Mexico to the Canadian border.

Nomadic—People who don't live in one place. They travel all the time, usually following animal herds, which they hunt for food.

Oregon Trail—A trail used by settlers and wagon trains beginning in the early 1840s. The trail began in Missouri, went through Nebraska along the Platte River, and then on toward Oregon.

Oto—Also spelled Otoe, this is a Native American tribe that lived in Nebraska before the arrival of the Europeans. They were one of the first tribes encountered by the Lewis and Clark Expedition (1804-1806) exploring the lands west of the Mississippi River.

Ponca—A Native American tribe that lived in northwest Nebraska. Chief Standing Bear (1829-1908) became famous for winning a court case against the United States government.

Reservation—Land set aside by the United States federal government for Native Americans.

Transcontinental Railroad—An American railroad line that stretched from the Atlantic Ocean to the Pacific Ocean, across the continent.

Index